NEW CARISSA

The Ship That Refused To Die

Written & Illustrated by
Steven Michael Smith

AuthorHouse™
1663 Liberty Drive
Bloomington, IN 47403
www.authorhouse.com
Phone: 1-800-839-8640

First published by AuthorHouse 10/27/2010

ISBN: 978-1-4520-6612-7 (sc)

Library of Congress Control Number: 2010912476

Printed in the United States of America

This book is printed on acid-free paper.

authorHOUSE®

DEDICATED TO
Family and Friends for all their support.

A SPECIAL THANKS TO
The Coos County Cultural Coalition, Oregon
and
3B's Nursery and Gardening Coos Bay, Oregon

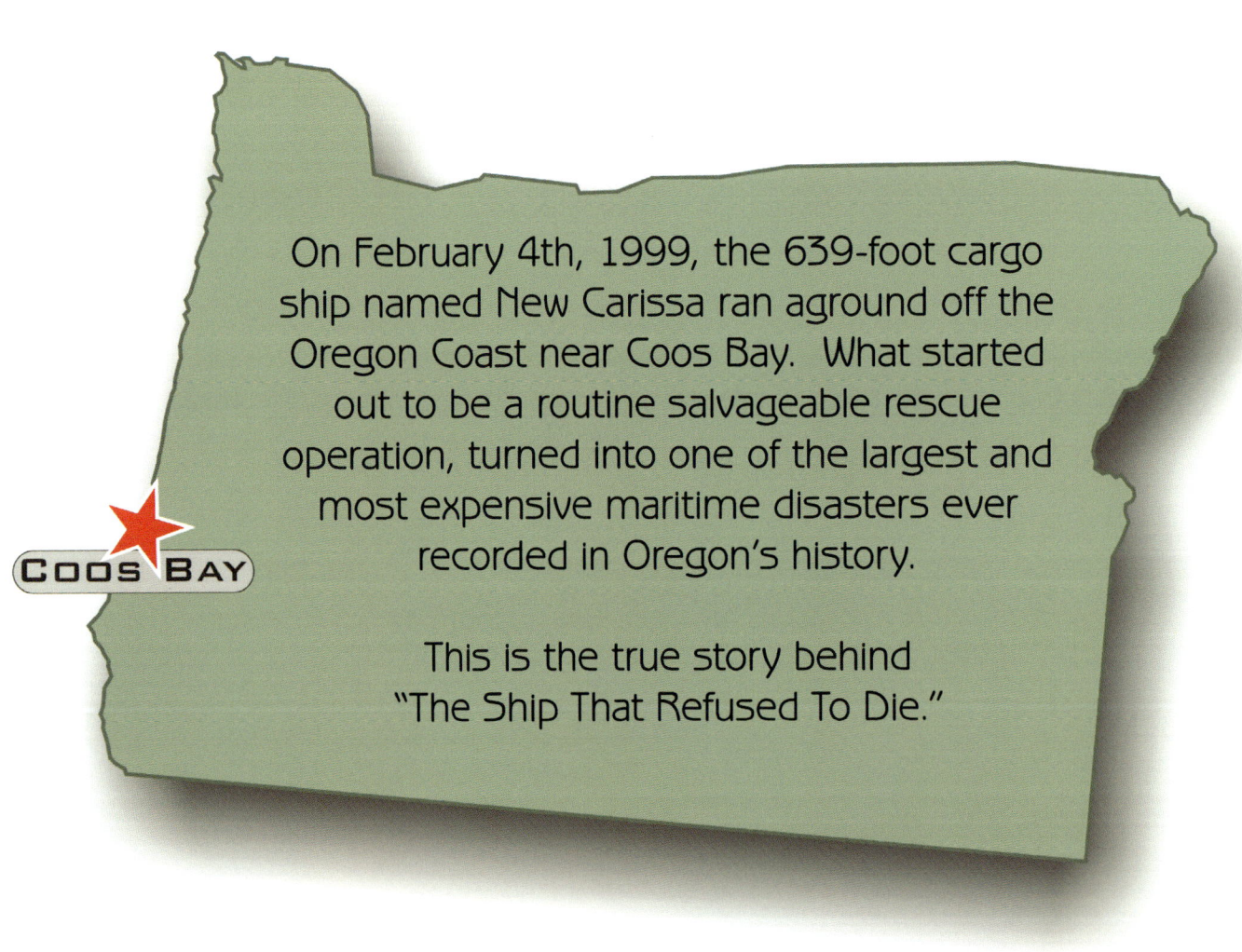

On February 4th, 1999, the 639-foot cargo ship named New Carissa ran aground off the Oregon Coast near Coos Bay. What started out to be a routine salvageable rescue operation, turned into one of the largest and most expensive maritime disasters ever recorded in Oregon's history.

This is the true story behind "The Ship That Refused To Die."

Coos Bay

KEY WORDS TO KNOW

New Carissa............Was a Panamanian-flagged bulk cargo ship and owned by a Japanese shipping company.

Bow...(bou)...............The forward end of a boat or ship.

Stern...(sturn)...........The rear end of a boat or ship.

Unified Command......A joint command that is composed of three services with the same ending goal. The New Carissa's Unified Command consisted of Coast Guard, Salvage crews, and environmental representatives.

Napalm.(NAY-pam).....A thickener consisting of a mixture of aluminum soaps used in jelling gasoline.

USS David R. Ray.....The Navy destroyer used in the 1999 New Carissa "saga". In February of 2002, the USS David R. Ray was decommissioned. In June of 2008, the ex-David R. Ray was taken to Hawaii to be used as target practice. The New Carissa lasted longer than the USS David R. Ray.

USS Bremerton.........The nuclear powered submarine used in the 1999 New Carissa "saga".

Mark 48....................A $2.5 million dollar heavyweight torpedo designed to combat fast, deep-diving submarines and high performance surface ships.

International Bird Rescue Research Center...
(IBRRC) The leading authority in bird care and oil spill response since 1971.

On a cold dark rainy February night, the wind blew.

The ocean tossed and turned and became very angry.

After the storm passed, the coastal Oregon town of Coos Bay woke up to find a large ship stuck on the beach.

The ship rocked back and forth in the heavy surf.
Fuel began to leak from cracks forming on the ship's side.

The Coast Guard swiftly air lifted the crew to safety.

News reporters came from all over to report the story.

"*This morning, February 4th, 1999, the ship New Carissa, beached itself along the Southern Oregon Coast. It is unclear at this time what caused the accident,*" announced the reporter.

Salvage officials known as the Unified Command,
held an emergency town meeting.

"*To avoid an environmental disaster, we've got to burn the oil off
the ship, and burn it now! It's the only way,*" the salvage consultant
reported. "*The next storm will definitely break up the ship for sure!*"

In a daring attempt, never done before in the lower 48 states, a U.S. Navy Explosive Team from Washington State came down and set explosive fire to the doomed ship.

Experts were hoping the fire would burn off the oil and prevent an environmental disaster. The explosives were not powerful enough, and the first attempt failed.

On the following night...the ground trembled.

KABOOM!

A huge fireball shot hundreds of feet into the night sky. Thick black smoke poured from the doomed New Carissa.

The heat and fire from the explosion broke the ship into two pieces. The fire was the largest planned burn in United States history used on a ship stranded in water.

The storm officials tried to beat didn't come, but the oil spill they feared did. An estimated 70,000 gallons of oil leaked into the ocean.

Cleanup crews were called to clean up the sticky
oil that was spilling on the beaches.

The day was known as **"Black Monday."**

Sick birds covered in the sticky oil were taken to the bird rehabilitation center.

The birds were cleaned and checked by the International Bird Rescue Teams.

Rescue workers could only wait and hope for the best.

The Safety Officer for the Unified Command was called in to protect the workers and to keep curious sightseers at a safe distance.

"*This is as close as you can get,*" he'd warn.
"*It's for your own safety.*"

The fuel was too cold and too thick to keep burning on its own.

So, a helicopter was used to drop flaming jellied petroleum, or napalm, into the fuel tanks to keep the oil burning. Black choking smoke poured from the freighter.

However, this idea didn't work very well.

"*Now what do we do?,*" the officials wondered.

Another violent storm
was coming and there was still a lot of oil on the ship.

An emergency meeting was held right on the beach.
"*Let's pump the oil off the ship,*" an official suggested.

Officials cut a hole in the side of the ship and placed a hose in the tanks.

They tried pumping the oil to trucks on the beach, but
the oil was still too cold and too thick. Failure again.
Time was running out!

The Unified Command was
out of workable options.

They made the desperate decision to tow
the larger section of the ship off the beach,
and sink it two hundred miles out at sea.

Once connected with a special towline from Holland, the little tug, named Sea Victory, started pulling on the bow section of the New Carissa.

The tug pulled and pulled...but the New Carissa's bow wouldn't budge.

The little tug tried again. It pulled and pulled...and finally the New Carissa's bow moved an encouraging thirty five feet.

Twenty six days after getting stuck in the sand near Coos Bay, the bow section of the New Carissa drifted westward over a final sandbar and started on its final voyage to be sunk out at sea.

The Unified Command waved "bon voyage" to the New Carissa, and they raised their hands in a symbol of victory.

"We did it," cheered the Salvage Consultant. *"Finally a bit of luck,"* proclaimed the Coast Guard Chief. *"We were successful,"* shouted the Environmental Officer.

Once again the bow of the New Carissa had other plans.

The ship's bow had been towed into the path of hurricane force winds and heavy seas. The ocean pounded the little tug and the New Carissa.

"Mayday! Mayday!"

The special towline connecting the tug to the ship broke. The little tug lost control and the New Carissa was floating loose in the water.

The Coast Guard Chief said, "*Certainly the worst thing to happen would be that the ship would come up on shore again.*"

He was right. The worst thing that could happen did.
The bow of the New Carissa drifted back to shore.

A small Oregon Coast town by the name of Waldport, 75 miles north of Coos Bay, was surprised to wake up to find the bow of the New Carissa grounded on their beach.

News reporters followed the New Carissa to Waldport.

"Same ship, new nightmare," announced a reporter. *"Mother nature has a mind of her own and apparently so does the New Carissa."*

Not only did the New Carissa's bow and reporters show up on the beach in Waldport, but so did the oil.

The disaster showing up on their beach made the residents of Waldport very angry.

Residents protested against the arrival of the New Carissa.

"*You're polluting our beach!*" Shouted one.
"*How could YOU let an accident happen twice?*" Questioned another.
"*Who is responsible for this mess?*" They all wanted to know.

Cleanup crews dotted the beach in front of the New Carissa's bow. They frantically worked day and night to make sure no oil was left on the beach.

Several days later, the little tug pulled the bow of the New Carissa off the beach, just as the sun was setting.

Again, the plan was to sink the bow 200 miles off the Oregon Coast.

Once far out at sea the Navy destroyer, USS David R. Ray, from San Diego, California came and shot 69 holes into the side of the New Carissa.

Officials were hoping the holes would let trapped
air escape, and allow seawater to enter the ship,
causing the New Carissa's bow to sink.
This plan failed too. The New Carissa refused to go down.

So another desperate attempt was made.

The USS Bremerton, a nuclear-powered submarine from Pearl Harbor Hawaii, came and fired a "Mark 48" torpedo at the bow of the New Carissa. The power of the impact lifted the ship up out of the water.

This time, the New Carissa wasn't able to fight against the powerful attack of the torpedo.

On March 11, 1999, thirty-six days after running aground in Coos Bay, the bow of the New Carissa drifted off into a fog bank and slowly sank.

Meanwhile, the stern section of the New Carissa remained partially buried in the sand on the beach where it originally grounded near Coos Bay.

Thousands of visitors from hundreds of miles away came to see what was left of the now famous and very stubborn New Carissa.

The New Carissa quickly became a star. Everybody wanted to get their picture taken with the ship that refused to die.

Eventually the crowds left.

The top half of the New Carissa's stern section was slowly
dismantled and the pieces recycled.

The New Carissa proved to be a survivor. The ship was:

beached...

burned...

broken...

towed...

beached again...

protested against...

towed again...

shot at...

torpedoed...

stuck...

visited...

and dismantled,

yet through all the New Carissa experienced, the ship remained stuck on the Oregon Coast!

Several attempts were made in the summers of 1999, 2000, and 2001 to tow the stern section of the New Carissa out to sea and sink it.

Everything they tried failed.

Officials didn't know what else to do to safely remove what remained of the New Carissa from the Oregon Coast.

On November 12th, 2002, the courts ruled that the two remaining pieces of the New Carissa were "negligent of trespassing."

The owners of the ship were fined 25 million dollars, to be paid to the State of Oregon.

The New Carissa taught officials a harsh lesson that dealing with a modern-day shipwreck can be a costly, complicated, and embarrassing undertaking.

What remained of the New Carissa was successfully dismantled,
and completely removed from the Oregon
Coast during the summer of 2008.

It took nine challenging years to get rid of the New Carissa.
"The Ship That Refused To Die."

The End.

NEW CARISSA

~ Time Line ~

Feb 4, 1999: *The 639-foot New Carissa* went aground in a storm near Coos Bay, Oregon.

Feb. 6, 1999: Bill Milwee, the salvage expert on the New Carissa spill response command team, says, "*We have no fear. We'll get it out of here.*"

Feb. 8 1999: The ship begins leaking from two of its five fuel oil tanks. Crews begin deploying cleanup equipment.

Feb. 11, 1999: The Navy team sets the ship ablaze. Hours later, the stern section splits apart from the bow. For several days, crews try to reignite the remaining fuel.

Mar. 2, 1999: The New Carissa heads to sea, but about 40 miles out, the towline snaps during one of the worst storms of the winter.

Mar. 3, 1999: The New Carissa's bow runs aground near Waldport about sunrise and begins leaking oil again.

Mar. 8, 1999: The Sea Victory tug yanks the bow off the beach again and heads to sea.

March 11, 1999: After the Navy destroyer, the *USS David R. Ray,* failed to sink the bow with explosives and artillery shells, the Navy submarine, *USS Bremerton,* fires a "Mark 48" torpedo, and sank the bow.

June 5, 1999: Crews begin dismantling parts of the stern.

Oct. 5, 1999: The Salvage Chief hooks lines to the stern then tried to tow it to a burial site 46 miles offshore, but all attempts failed. The stern still remained on the beach.

November 13, 2002: In a 10-2 ruling, a Coos County jury found the owners of the New Carissa guilty of negligent trespass and awarded Oregon $25 million to pay for removing the ship's stern.

March 2008: Titan Maritime, a worldwide marine salvage and shipwreck company, begins work on removing the wreckage; work continues through the summer and fall.

September 23, 2008: The last visible piece of the wreck was lifted out of the water. By September 28 the pieces remaining on the ocean floor were successfully removed by the Titan Company.

Though the environmental impact was devastating for the Oregon Coast, the oil spill from the New Carissa shipwreck was quite small in comparison to other oil spills in the United States.

Exxon Valdez, Alaska ~ March 24, 1989
10.8 million gallons

New Carissa, Oregon ~ February 4, 1999
70 thousand gallons

Deepwater Horizon Gulf Spill ~ June 25, 2010
Approximately 220 million gallons

Lightning Source UK Ltd.
Milton Keynes UK
UKIC01n2235180615
253780UK00008B/50